D0890006

THE TRIALS
OF
PHILLIS
WHEATLEY

THE TRIALS OF PHILLIS WHEATLEY

*AMERICA'S FIRST BLACK POET
AND HER ENCOUNTERS WITH
THE FOUNDING FATHERS*

HENRY LOUIS GATES, JR.

BASIC
CIVITAS
BOOKS

A Member of the Perseus Books Group

Published by Basic *Civitas* Books,
A Member of the Perseus Books Group

Library of Congress Cataloging-in-Publication Data

Gates, Henry Louis.
The trials of Phillis Wheatley / Henry Louis Gates, Jr.
p. cm.
ISBN 0-465-02729-6
1. Wheatley, Phillis, 1753-1784. 2. Poets, American--
Colonial period, ca. 1600-1775--Biography. 3. Women
slaves--United States--Biography. 4. African American
poets--Biography. I. Title.

PS866.W5Z595 2003
811'.1--dc21
2003002717

03 04 05 / 10 9 8 7 6 5 4 3 2 1

For

Sharon, Maggie, and Liza

ACKNOWLEDGMENTS

I would like to thank the National Council on the Humanities and William Ferris, chairman of the National Endowment for the Humanities, for selecting me to deliver the 2002 Jefferson Lecture and Bruce Cole, Dr. Ferris's successor, for his generous introduction to my lecture and for his kindness and hospitality to me and my family during our stay in Washington, and my visit with the staff at the endowment. To be chosen to deliver the Jefferson Lecture is a signal honor in a humanist's career. It most certainly was in mine, and I was deeply honored and humbled by my selection.

Several friends and colleagues aided me enormously both as I prepared the lecture and the longer essay that grew from the lecture. Jennifer Wood-Nangombe and Terri Oliver helped me to locate secondary sources on Wheatley, Jefferson, and Wheatley's eighteen "authenticators." John Stauffer pointed me to the writings of several black abolitionists who wrote about Thomas Jefferson. Vincent Carretta kindly lent his considerable expertise on Wheatley and her world as I completed my manuscript, and William Andrews helped me to understand Wheatley in the larger context of slave literature. Dana Goodyear and Henry Finder provided remarkably generous editorial advice as I revised the lecture for publication in *The New Yorker*. Homi Bhabha, Ted Widmer, and Argela DeLeon offered valuable comments on the working draft. Hollis Robbins aided me enormously in editing the various versions of this essay and arriving at a final text. Abby Wolf checked my bibliographical sources and helped me to compile the bibliography. Elizabeth Maguire expressed support for the publication of my Jefferson Lecture as a book almost as soon as it was delivered, and her assistant, Will Morrison Garland, helped me to adhere to a strict set of deadlines. Joanne Kendall, as always, typed the several drafts of the text. William Ferris, former chair of the endowment, extended the invitation to deliver the Jefferson Lecture, while his successor, Bruce Cole, assisted ably by his colleague, Mary Lou Beatty, presided graciously and efficiently over the lecture and the ceremonies surrounding it. I would especially like to thank my wife, Sharon Adams, for her enthusiasm for this project, and her patience as I struggled to complete this meditation on Phillis Wheatley's importance to her own time, and ours.

PREFACE

This book is an expanded version of the Thomas Jefferson Lecture in the Humanities that I was privileged to deliver to the Library of Congress in March 2002. I would like to express my deepest appreciation to the National Endowment for the Humanities, its past chairman William R. Ferris, its current chairman, Bruce Cole, and the National Council on the Humanities for choosing me to deliver the Jefferson Lecture on the thirtieth anniversary of the series.

The Jefferson Lectures began in 1972 with Lionel Trilling's address on "Mind in the Modern World." As hard as it is to believe, the

Jefferson Lectures are more than a tenth as old as the nation they serve. I am honored to occupy a line of succession that includes Saul Bellow, Walker Percy, Toni Morrison, John Hope Franklin, and so many other luminaries.

It is humbling to receive what has been called the highest intellectual honor bestowed by the U.S. government. I feel especially humbled and appreciative because I interpret this honor as a statement about my field, African-American studies, which arrived in the academy only three decades ago.

I am especially proud to be a fellow countryman of Jefferson's in several senses. As a citizen, like all of you, of the republic of letters. As an American who believes deeply in the soaring promise of the Declaration of Independence. As a native of Piedmont, West Virginia, and, hence, in a broad sense, a fellow Virginian.

Who knows? Judging from all the DNA disclosures of the last few years, I may even be related to him. For all of us, white and black alike, Jefferson remains an essential ancestor.

John F. Kennedy once famously addressed a group of distinguished intellectuals by saying they were the greatest gathering of brilliant thinkers to visit the White House since Jefferson dined alone. It's a great line—but I don't think Jefferson ever did dine alone. Even when no one was at the table with him, someone was cooking for him, someone was bringing him his food, and somebody was busy planning his next meal. And the chances are good that some of those people were African Americans. And it is Jefferson's role in the shaping of black literary and political discourse that is the subject of this book.

I hope that readers will accept my challenge to recuperate Phillis Wheatley, the first African poet in English, from the long shadow of Jefferson's misgivings about her gifts.

Henry Louis Gates, Jr.
Cambridge, MA
February 19, 2003

The Trials of
Phillis Wheatley

It was the primal scene of African-American letters. Sometime before October 8, 1772, Phillis Wheatley, a slim, African slave in her late teens, met with eighteen gentlemen so august that they could later allow themselves to be identified publicly "as the most respectable characters in Boston." The panel had been assembled to verify the authorship of her poems and to answer a much larger question: was a Negro capable of producing literature?

The details of the meeting have been lost to history, but I have often imagined how it might have happened. She entered the room—perhaps in Boston's Town Hall, the Old Colony House—carrying a manuscript consisting of twenty-odd poems that she claims to have written. No doubt the young woman would have been demure, soft-spoken, and frightened, for she was about to undergo one of the oddest oral examinations on record, one that would determine the course of her life and the fate of her work, and one that, ultimately, would determine whether she remained a slave or would be set free. The stakes, in other words, were as high as they could get for an oral exam. She is on trial and so is her race.

She would have been familiar with the names of the gentlemen assembled in this room. For there, perhaps gathered in a semi-circle, would have sat an astonishingly influential group of the colony's citizens determined to satisfy for themselves, and thus put to rest, fundamental questions about the authenticity of this woman's literary achievements. Their interrogation of this witness, and her answers, would determine not only this woman's fate but the subsequent direction of the antislavery movement, as well as the birth of what a later commentator would call "a new species of literature," the literature written by slaves.

Who would this young woman have confronted that day in the early autumn of 1772? At the center no doubt would have sat His Excellency Thomas Hutchinson, the governor of Massachusetts. Hutchinson, a colonial historian and a royal official, who would end his life in England as a loyalist refugee, was born in Boston into a wealthy family descended from merchants. (Anne Hutchinson was also an ancestor.) Young Thomas, we are told, preferred "reading history to playing with other children" and early on became an admirer of Charles I. So precocious was he that he entered Harvard College at the age of twelve, "where," his biographer tells us, "his social standing entitled him to be ranked third in his class." (Even back then, grade inflation loomed on the banks of the Charles River.)

Hutchinson was the governor between 1769 and 1774. Following the Boston Tea Party, Hutchinson went to London "for consultations." His family joined him in exile in 1776. Just four years following this examination, he would receive an honorary degree from the University of Oxford on, of all days, July 4, 1776. Hutchinson never returned to his beloved estate in Milton, Massachusetts.

At Hutchinson's side in the makeshift seminar room would have sat Andrew Oliver, the colony's lieutenant governor (and Hutchinson's brother-in-law through his wife's sister). Oliver, who took the A.B. and M.A. degrees from Harvard, became—along with his brother and business partners, Peter and Thomas Hutchinson—leaders of the faction that dominated provincial Massachusetts politics until the eve of the Revolution. Oliver imprudently allowed himself to be publicly identified as a supporter of the Stamp Act of

1765, prompting angry crowds to ransack his house and uproot his garden. When in 1774, Oliver died of a stroke, commentators assumed it to have been brought on by the increasingly vituperative attacks of the antiloyalists.

Quite a few men of the cloth were present. The Reverend Mather Byles, still another Harvard graduate, taking the A.B. degree in 1725 and his A.M. in 1728, was the first and only minister of the Hollis Street Congregational Church in Boston between 1732 and 1775. Byles was the grandson of Increase Mather and the nephew of Cotton Mather. As a young man Byles corresponded with Alexander Pope and Isaac Watts, and in 1744 he had published his own book of verse, *Poems on Several Occasions*. Byles was highly regarded for his wit; his sermons "praised for their sonorous language and elaborate descriptive passages," Mary Rhinelander McCarl tells us, and "not for their probing ethical, moral, or theological content." He was a favorite for delivering eulogies at state funerals. Like Hutchinson and Oliver, Byles was a Tory loyalist, and he lost his pulpit when Massachusetts finally rebelled. He was sentenced to banishment, later committed to house arrest, for his loyalist views. (Ever the wit, he called the sentry stationed just outside of his home his "Observe-a-Tory.")

Besides Mather Byles, another poet was there that morning: Joseph Green, a well-known satirist. David Robinson calls Green "the foremost wit of his day," and he and Byles often exchanged satiric poems and parodies. Among Green's most well-known pieces was a lampoon of Boston's first Masonic procession, held in 1749, and entitled *Entertainment for a Winter's Evening*. The poem depicts the Masons as proceeding from church to their real destination, a tavern. A loyalist to the end, Green fled to London in 1775; he died in exile in 1880.

The Reverend Samuel Cooper, also a poet, received his A.B. and A.M. from Harvard in

1743 and 1746, respectively. He was the only minister of the Brattle Street Church from 1747 until his death in 1783. Known as "the silver-tongued preacher," Cooper was Minister to no less than "one-fourth of Boston's merchants and more than half of Boston's selectmen," as Frederick V. Mills tells us. Mills continues: "Cooper was at the center of an inner circle consisting of James Otis, John Hancock, James Bowdoin, Joseph Warren and Samuel Adams, who showed outward respect for Governor Thomas Hutchinson at the same time they kept agitation against British policy focused." So pivotal was Cooper's role during the Revolution in encouraging the American alliance with France in 1777 that he would receive a stipend from Louis XVI until his death.

The august James Bowdoin was included in this circle of inquisition as well. Bowdoin was one of the principal American exemplars of the Enlightenment. A close friend of Franklin's, he was a student of electricity and astronomy, as well as a poet, publishing a volume titled *A Paraphrase on Part of the Oeconomy of Human Life* in 1759, and four poems in the volume *Harvard Verses* presented to George III in 1762 "in an attempt to gain royal patronage for the struggling college," as Gordon E. Kershaw notes. His remarkable library contained 1,200 volumes, ranging in subjects from science and math to philosophy, religion, poetry and fiction. By the time of this interview, he had become a vocal opponent of Governor Hutchinson's policies. Bowdoin would become the governor of Massachusetts in 1776. In addition to opposing the policies of the royalists in the room, Bowdoin was also a steadfast foe of "his old political enemy," John Hancock, who was also in the room.

Like Bowdoin, Hancock prepared for Harvard at Boston Latin, then graduated from Harvard in the class of 1754, the second youngest in a class of twenty, in which he ranked fifth, William Fowler notes, as "an indication of his family's prominence." (His uncle, Thomas—his guardian after age eight—was one of Boston's wealthiest merchants, and John was raised in a Beacon Hill mansion.) Upon his uncle's death in 1764, John assumed the leadership of the House of Hancock, which grew rich by trafficking in whale oil and real estate. In part because the Sugar Act of 1764 and the Stamp Act of 1765 had such dire effects on business, and because he resented what he saw as an abridgement of his rights as an Englishman, Hancock increasingly identified his interests with the patriots, both as a Boston selectman and member of the General Court. Hancock became something of a hero in patriot circles when, in 1768, his sloop, the *Liberty*, was seized for smuggling Madeira. The Sons of Liberty organized a mob, which attacked the customs officials, who then fled for their lives. Hancock was hailed as a victor over British oppression, and would go on to become the third president of the Continental Congress, and the first governor of the Commonwealth.

The Reverend Samuel Mather, son of Cotton Mather, graduated from Harvard College in 1723. He was Thomas Hutchinson's brother-in-law. Mather's career as a minister was quite controversial—he was charged with "improper conduct" in 1741, and, though found innocent, was dismissed that same year from his pulpit at the Second Church in Boston. (Misbehavior among Boston clerics was regarded less leniently than would later be the case!) Mather is principally remembered for his library, which Mason I. Lowance describes as "one of the greatest in New England." But he is also remembered, Lowance concludes, as being "the end of that dynasty" that had commenced with his great-grandfather Richard in 1630.

What an astounding collection of people were gathered in the room that morning—relations and rivals, friends and foes. Here truly was a plenum of talent and privilege, cultivation and power. There were seven ordained ministers, three poets, six staunch loyalists, and several signal figures in the battle for independence. Of these eighteen gentlemen, many were Harvard graduates.

What they were not, however, was an association for the advancement of colored people. Of the eighteen gentlemen assembled, a majority were slaveholders: one, Thomas Hubbard, had actually been a dealer in slaves. Even the venerable James Bowdoin bought and sold slaves in the 1760s, while we know from Joseph Green's will that he left one hundred pounds to his slave "Plato." Another, the Reverend Charles Chauncy, in 1743, had attacked the Great Awakening because it allowed "women and girls; yea Negroes—to do the business of preachers."

Five among them—Bowdoin, Cooper, Hubbard, Moorhead, and Oliver—would be immortalized by the poet herself either in elegies upon their deaths or occasional verse. In the hands of this group, self-constituted as judge and jury, rested the fate of Phillis Wheatley, and to a large extent the destiny of the African-

American literary tradition, on that October day in 1772.

Why had this august tribunal been assembled by John Wheatley, Phillis's master? They had one simple charge: to determine whether Phillis Wheatley was truly the author of the poems she claimed to have written. John Wheatley hoped that they would support Phillis's claim of authorship, and that the opinion of the general public would follow.

And to understand how fraught this moment was, we need to turn from the judges to the one they were judging.

The girl who came to be known as Phillis Wheatley came to town on July 11, 1761, on board a schooner, the *Phillis*, owned by Timothy Finch and captained by Peter Gwinn. The ship had recently returned from gathering slaves in Senegal, Sierra Leone, and the Isles de Los, off the coast of Guinea. Among its cargo was "a slender frail, female child," a Wheatley relative would write, "supposed to have been about seven years old, at this time, from the circumstances of shedding her front teeth." It's a fair guess that she would have been a native Wolof speaker from the Senegambian coast. Mrs. Susanna Wheatley, wife of the prosperous tailor and merchant, John Wheatley, in response to advertisements in the *Boston Evening Post* and the *Boston Gazette and Country Journal* in July and August, went to the schooner to purchase a house servant. Mrs. Wheatley acquired the child at the wharf on Beach Street "for a trifle," one of her descendants tells us, "as the captain had fears of her dropping off his hands, without emolument, by death." The child was "naked," covered only by "a quantity of dirty carpet about her like a fillibeg."

The two boarded "the chaise of her mistress" and returned to the Wheatley mansion located on the corner of King Street and Mackerel Lane (today's State and Kilby Streets), just a few blocks from the Old State House. Both the Stamp Act riots of 1765 and the Boston Massacre of 1770 took place down the street from her front door. Wheatley's loving biographer, William Robinson, estimates her purchase price as less than ten pounds. Susanna Wheatley named the child "Phillis," ironically enough, after the name of the schooner that had brought her from Africa.

According to Robinson, Phillis's Boston consisted of 15,520 people in 1765, 1,000 of whom were black. Of this black population only eighteen, as of 1762, were free. Between Phillis's arrival in 1761 and her death in 1784, "no black children," Robinson continues, "could be counted among the more than 800 young scholars enrolled in the city's two grammar or Latin schools and the three vocational writing schools."

John and Susanna Wheatley had teenaged twins, Nathaniel and Mary, who were living at home when Phillis arrived. For reasons never explained, Mary, apparently with her mother's enthusiastic encouragement, began to teach the child slave to read. (Mary would marry the Reverend John Lathrop, known as "the Revolutionary Preacher," and pastor of the Old North Church.) Phillis, by all accounts, was a keen and quick pupil. As Lathrop wrote to a friend in 1773, his wife had "taught her to read, and by seeing others use the pen, she learned to write." Mary tutored Phillis in English, Latin, and the Bible. William Robinson aptly calls her "rewardingly precocious." That, if anything, is an understatement. As John Wheatley wrote in 1772 of her intellect and progress in letters:

Phillis was brought from Africa to America, in the Year 1761, between Seven and Eight years of Age. Without any Assistance from School Education, and by only what she was taught in the Family, she, in sixteen Months Time from her Arrival, attained the English Language, to which she was an utter Stranger before, to such a Degree, as to read any, most difficult Parts of

the Sacred Writings to the great Astonish-
ment of all who heard her.

As to her Writing, her own Curiosity led
her to it; and this she learnt in so short a
time, that in the Year 1765, she wrote a letter to the Reverend Mr. Occom, the Indian
Minister, while in England.

She has a great Inclination to learn the
Latin tongue, and has made some progress in
it. This Relation is given by her Master who
bought her, and with whom she now lives.

Recall that this seven-year-old slave spoke
no English upon her arrival in 1761. By
1765, she had written her first poem; in
1767, when she was thirteen or fourteen, the
Newport Mercury published a poem that Susanna Wheatley submitted on her behalf. In
1770, when she was about seventeen, she immortalized the Boston Massacre in her
poem, "On the Affray in King Street, on the
Evening of the 5th of March, 1770." It reads
in part:

Long as in Freedom's Cause the wise contend,
Dear to your unity shall Fame extend;
While to the World, the letter's Stone shall
    tell,
How Caldwell, Attucks, Gray, and
    Mav'rick fell.

That same year, her elegy on the death of the Reverend George Whitefield—the widely popular English preacher, leader of the evangelical movement, and favorite of Susanna Wheatley—was published within weeks of his sudden and untimely death during a speaking tour in America. This exceptionally popular poem was published as a broadside in Boston, then again in Newport, four more times in Boston, and a dozen more in New York, Philadelphia, and Newport. Advertisements for the broadside appeared in "more than a dozen newspapers in Pennsylvania, New York, and Boston, and at least ten times in Boston newspapers alone." Whitefield had been the chaplain of an English philanthropist, Selina Hastings, the countess of Huntingdon. Wheatley shrewdly apostrophized the countess in the Whitefield elegy, and sent a letter of condolence with the poem enclosed. With the poem's subsequent publication in London in 1771, Wheatley suddenly had a wide readership on both sides of the Atlantic. It made her the Toni Morrison of her time.

Delighted with her slave's dazzling abilities and her growing fame, Susanna Wheatley set out to have Phillis's work collected and published as a book. Advertised in the Tory paper, the Boston *Censor*, on February 29, March 14, and April 18, 1772, was a list of the titles of twenty-eight poems that would make up Wheatley's first book, if enough subscribers— perhaps 300—could be found to underwrite the cost of publication. But the necessary number of subscribers could not be found because not enough Bostonians could believe that an African slave possessed the requisite degree of reason and wit to write a poem by herself.

To understand why Wheatley's achievement prompted such incredulity, it helps to know something about the broader discourse of race and reason in the eighteenth century. To summarize a vast and complex body of literature, involving Francis Bacon, David Hume, Immanuel Kant, and Georg Frederick Hegel, many philosophers of the Renaissance and the Enlightenment were vexed by the question of what kind of creatures Africans truly were— that is, were they human beings, descended along with Europeans from a common ancestor and fundamentally related to other human beings, or were they, as Hume put it in 1753, another "species of men," related more to apes than to Europeans? As Hume wrote:

I am apt to suspect the Negroes, and in general all the other species of men (for there are four or five different kinds) to be naturally inferior to the whites. There never was a civilized nation of any other complexion than white, nor even any indi-

vidual eminent either in action or specula-
tion. No ingenious manufacturers amongst
them, no arts, no sciences.

Such a uniform and constant difference
could not happen, in so many countries
and ages, if nature had not made an original distinction betwixt these breeds of
men. Not to mention our colonies, there
are Negro slaves dispersed all over Europe, of which none ever discovered any
symptoms of ingenuity; tho' low people,
without education, will start up amongst
us, and distinguish themselves in every
profession. In Jamaica indeed they talk of
one Negro as a man of parts and learning
[Francis Williams]; but 'tis likely he is ad-
mired for very slender accomplishment,
like a parrot, who speaks a few words
plainly.

Just ten years later, Kant, responding di-
rectly to Hume, expanded upon his observations:

The Negroes of Africa have by nature no feeling that rises above the trifling. Mr. Hume challenges anyone to cite a single example in which a Negro has shown talents, and asserts that among the hundreds of thousands of blacks who are transported elsewhere from the countries, although many of them have been set free, still not a single one was ever found who presented anything great in art or science or any other praiseworthy quality, even though among the whites some continually rise aloft from the lowest rabble, and through superior gifts earn respect in the world. So fundamental is the difference between these two races of man, and it appears to be as great in regard to mental capacities as in color.

The question of whether Africans were human was less related to color than the possession of reason, a tradition inaugurated by Descartes. But how was the faculty of reason to be recognized? Increasingly after Hume voiced his doubts about the African's capacity to create "arts and sciences," the question turned on whether or not Africans could write, that is, could create imaginative literature. If they could, this line of reasoning went, then they stood as members of the human family on the Great Chain of Being. If they could not, then the Africans were a species sub-human, more related to the apes than to Europeans. Even Thomas Jefferson had associated Africans with apes: black males find white women more beautiful than black women, Jefferson had argued, "as uniformly as is the preference of the Oranootan for the black woman over his own species." As the Reverend Robert Nickol would put it in 1788, "I have not heard that an ourang outang has composed an ode."

All of this helps us to understand why Wheatley's oral examination was so important. If she had indeed written her poems, then this would demonstrate that Africans were human beings and should be liberated from slavery. If, on the other hand, she had not written, or could not write her poems, or if indeed she was like a parrot who speaks a few words plainly, then that would be another matter entirely. Essentially, she was auditioning for the humanity of the entire African people.

Some of the most skeptical had already conducted their own examinations of Phillis, one-on-one. Thomas Woolbridge, an emissary of the earl of Dartmouth, was among those who visited the Wheatley mansion. Woolbridge wrote to Dartmouth about his encounter:

> While in Boston, I heard of a very Extraordinary female Slave, who made some verses on our mutually dear deceased Friend [Whitefield]; I visited her mistress, and found by conversing with the African, that she was no Imposter; I asked if she could write on any Subject; she said Yes;

we had just heard of your Lordships Appointment; I gave her your name, which she was well acquainted with. She, immediately, wrote a rough Copy of the inclosed Address & Letter, which I promised to convey or deliver. I was astonished, and could hardly believe my own Eyes. I was present when she wrote, and can attest that it is her own production; she shewd me her Letter to Lady Huntington [sic], which, I dare say, Your Lordship has seen; I send you an Account signed by her master of her Importation, Education &.c They are all wrote in her own hand.

Boston's reading public remained skeptical, however. As one of Phillis's supporters in Boston put it in a letter to his brother-in-law in Philadelphia, Wheatley's master "could not sell it by reason of their not crediting ye performances to be by a Negro."

And so the bold gambit in the Old Colony House—the decision to assemble some of the finest minds in all colonial America to question closely the African adolescent about the slender sheaf of twenty-eight poems that she and her master and mistress claimed that she had written by herself.

We have no transcript of the exchanges that occurred between Miss Wheatley and her eighteen examiners. But we can imagine that some of their questions would have been prompted on the classical allusions in Wheatley's poems. "Who was Apollo?" "What happened when Phaeton rode his father's chariot?" "How did Zeus give birth to Athena?" "Name the Nine Muses." Was she perhaps asked for an extemporaneous demonstration of her talent? What we do know is that she passed with flying colors. After interrogating the poet, the tribunal of eighteen agreed to sign the following attestation:

We whose Names are under-written, do assure the World, that the Poems specified in the following Page, were (as we verily believe) written by Phillis, a young Negro Girl, who was but a few Years since, brought an uncultivated Barbarian from Africa, and has ever since been, and now is, under the Disadvantage of serving as a Slave in a Family in this Town. She has been examined by some of the best Judges, and is thought qualified to write them.

That attestation was deemed absolutely essential to the publication of Wheatley's book, and even with the attestation no American publisher was willing to take on her manuscript. Susanna Wheatley turned to English friends for help. The publishing climate in England was more receptive to black authors. The Countess of Huntingdon though a slaveholder herself (she had inherited slaves in Georgia) had already, in 1772, shepherded into print one of the earliest slave narratives, by James Gronniosaw. Vincent Carretta, a leading scholar of eighteenth-century black transatlantic literature and an expert on Wheatley, has observed that the British market for black literature may have been indirectly created by a court ruling, in 1772, that made it illegal for slaves who had come to England to be forcibly returned to the colonies. Although the ruling stopped short of outlawing slavery in England, it encouraged an atmosphere of sympathy toward blacks.

Through the captain of the commercial ship that John Wheatley used for trade with England, Susanna engaged a London publisher, Archibald Bell, to bring out the manuscript. The countess agreed to let Wheatley dedicate the book to her. An engraving of Wheatley appeared as the book's frontpiece, at the countess's request.

And so, against the greatest odds, *Poems on Various Subjects, Religious and Moral* became the first book of poetry published by a person of African descent in the English language, marking the beginning of an African-American literary tradition. Various black

authors had published individual poems, but
even these instances were rare. Jupiter Hammon, a slave from Long Island, had published the first of several poems in 1760.
Edward Long caused a minor sensation when
he discovered in 1774 that Francis Williams,
a Jamaican who is said to have studied at the
University of Cambridge, had apparently in
1759 written an ode in Latin.

Five advertisements for the book in the
London Morning Post and *Advertiser in August*
all point to the statement from the esteemed
Bostonians as proof that Phillis is the volume's "real Author." What's more, everyone
knew that the publication of Wheatley's
book was an historical event, greeted by
something akin to the shock of cloning a
sheep. As her printer, Archibald Bell bluntly
put it in the same newspaper on September
13, 1773: "The book here proposed for publication displays perhaps one of the greatest
instances of pure, unassisted genius, that the
world ever produced." For, he continues,

"the Author is a native of Africa, and left not the dark part of the habitable system, till she was eight years old."

Given the context of the Enlightenment conversation on race and reason, it should come as no surprise that the book was widely reviewed and discussed in Europe and America. Even Voltaire was moved, in 1774, to write to a correspondent that Wheatley had proven that blacks could write poetry. John Paul Jones, on the eve of sailing to France in June 1777, on the newly commissioned warship, the *Ranger*, sent a note to a fellow officer, asking him to deliver a copy of some of his own enclosed writings to "the celebrated Phillis the African favorite of the Nine [Muses] and Apollo."

With the publication of her book, Phillis Wheatley, almost immediately, became the most famous African on the face of the earth, the Oprah Winfrey of her time. Phillis was the toast of London, where she had been sent with Nathaniel Wheatley in the spring of

1773 to oversee the publication of her book. There she met the Earl of Dartmouth, who gave her five guineas to buy the works of Alexander Pope; Granville Sharp, the scholar and antislavery activist, who took her to the Tower of London; and Brook Watson, a future Lord Mayor of London, who gave her a folio edition of "Paradise Lost." Benjamin Franklin paid her a visit, which he mentions in a letter to his nephew Jonathan Williams, Sr. "Upon your Recommendation I went to see the black Poetess and offer'd her any Services I could do her," he wrote. "And I have heard nothing since of her." On the strength of this seemingly perfunctory visit, Wheatley decided to dedicate her second volume of poetry to Franklin. Even an audience with King George was arranged, although she had to cancel it when Susanna Wheatley suddenly fell ill and needed her care.

Within a month of the book's publication and Phillis's return to America, the Wheatleys freed her. (English reviewers, using Wheatley's book as a point, had condemned the hypocrisy of a colony that insisted on liberty and equality when it came to its relationship to England but did not extend those principles to its own population.) "Freedom" meant that she became fully responsible for her literary career, and for her finances. In mid-October, she wrote a letter to David Wooster, the customs collector in New Haven, alerting him that a shipment of her books would soon arrive from England, and urging him to canvass among his friends for orders. "Use your interest with Gentlemen & Ladies of your acquaintance to subscribe also, for the more subscribers there are, the more it will be for my advantage as I am to have half the Sale of the Books." She continued, "This I am the more solicitous for, as I am now upon my own footing and whatever I get by this is entirely mine, & it is the Chief I have to depend upon. I must also request you would desire the Printers in New Haven, not to reprint that Book, as it will be a great hurt to me, preventing any further Benefit that I might receive from the Sale of my Copies from England."

Franklin was just one of four Founding Fathers who would cross Wheatley's path in one form or another. John Hancock was one of her interrogators. On October 26, 1775, Wheatley sent a letter and a poem she had written in his honor, to General George Washington at his headquarters in Cambridge. The letter reads as follows:

Sir [George Washington]

I have taken the freedom to address your Excellency in the enclosed poem, and entreat your acceptance, though I am not insensible of its inaccuracies. Your being appointed by the Grand Continental Congress to be Generalissimo of the armies of North America, together with the fame of your virtues, excite sensations not easy to suppress. Your generosity, therefore, I presume will pardon the attempt. Wishing your Excellency all possible success in the great cause you are so generously engaged in, I am,

Your Excellency's most humble servant,
Phillis Wheatley [October 26, 1775]

On February 28, 1776, Washington responded, acknowledging the gift of the poem and inviting Wheatley to visit him at his headquarters in Cambridge:

Miss Phillis,

Your favor of the 26th of October did not reach my hands, till the middle of December. Time enough, you will say, to have given an answer ere this. Granted. But a variety of important occurrences, continually interposing to distract the mind and withdraw the attention, I hope will apologize for the delay, and plead my excuse for the seeming but not real neglect. I thank you most sincerely for your polite notice of me, in the elegant lines you enclosed; and however undeserving I may be of such encomium and panegyric, the style and manner exhibit a striking proof of your poetical talents; in honor of which, and as a tribute justly due to you, I would have published the poem, had I not been apprehensive, that, while I only meant to give the world this new instance of your genius, I might have incurred the imputation of vanity. This, and nothing else, determined me not to give it place in the public prints.

If you should ever come to Cambridge, or near headquarters, I shall be happy to see a person so favored by the Muses, and to whom nature has so liberal and beneficent in her dispensations. I am, with great respect, your obedient humble servant.

According to Benson J. Lossing, "Washington invited her to visit him at Cambridge, which she did a few days before the British evacuated Boston. She passed half an hour with the commander-in-chief, from whom and his officers she received marked attention." Washington overcame his fear of the imputation of vanity and, by means of an intermediary, secured publication of Wheatley's pentametric praise in the *Virginia Gazette*, in March 1776. The poem is noteworthy in several ways, but especially for its description of Washington as "first in peace" and in its often repeated final couplet:

> One century scarce perform'd its destined
> round,
> When Gallic powers Columbia's fury found;
> And so may you, whoever dares disgrace
> The land of freedom's heaven-defended
> race! . . .

> Proceed, great chief, with virtue on thy side,
> Thy ev'ry action let the goddess guide.
> A crown, a mansion, and a throne that shine,
> With gold unfading, WASHINGTON! be
> thine.

But no encounter with a Founding Father would prove more lasting in its impact than that with Thomas Jefferson, whom she never met. (I should say that when we discuss the blind spots of giants like Jefferson, we must do so with the humility of knowing that, in future decades, others shall condescendingly be discussing our own blind spots, if they bother discussing us at all.)

Jefferson's literary criticism of Wheatley was occasioned by François, the Marquis de Barbé-Marbois, who inspired Jefferson's *Notes on the State of Virginia*. Marbois was, at the time, the secretary of the first French mission to the United States and later consul-general to the United States. In 1781, on behalf of his government, he had asked Jefferson for statistical information about various states in the Union, particularly Virginia. Jefferson sent his response to Marbois in 1781. Jefferson's report caused such a stir among Benjamin Rush and his fellows at the American Philosophical Society that he enlarged and revised his answers. A private edition of *Notes* was printed in Paris in 1785, an "authorized" edition was published by Stockdale in London in 1787, and the first American edition followed in 1788. Of Marbois's queries, it was that occasioned by his encounter with Wheatley's *Poems* in 1779, which proved germinal in the history of the criticism of African-American writing.

Marbois considered Phillis "one of the strangest creatures in the country and perhaps the whole world." In an August 28, 1779, journal entry subsequently sent to his fiancée in Paris, Marbois described Wheatley's accomplishments:

> Phyllis is a negress, born in Africa, brought to Boston at the age of ten, and sold to a citizen of the city. She learned English with unusual ease, eagerly read and re-read the Bible, the only book which had been put in her hands, became steeped in the poetic images of which it is full, and at the age of

seventeen, published a number of poems in which there is imagination, poetry, and zeal, though no correctness nor order nor interest. I read them with some surprise.

Jefferson begged to differ. In his response to his French correspondent's questions, as outlined in Queries VI and XIV of the *Notes*, Jefferson lays out clearly his views. "The compositions published under her name are below the dignity of criticism." The criticism comes in a passage setting out his views on the mental capacity of the various races of man. "In general, their existence appears to participate more of sensation than reflection," Jefferson writes about blacks; he continues:

> Comparing them by their faculties of memory, reason, and imagination, it appears to me that in memory they are equal to whites, in reason much inferior, as I think one could scarcely be found capable of tracing and comprehending the investi-

gations of Euclid; and that in imagination they are dull, tasteless, and anomalous.

Echoing Hume and Kant, he argues that blacks are exposed daily to "countries where the arts and sciences are cultivated to a considerable degree," yet they have absorbed little or nothing from this exposure. "Never yet," said Jefferson, "could I find that a black had uttered a thought above the level of plain narration, never see even an elementary trait of painting or sculpture." On the other hand, Jefferson has qualified praise for the African's musical propensities.

In music they are more generally gifted than the whites with accurate ears for tune and time, and they have been found capable of imagining a small catch. . . . Whether they will be equal to the composition of a more extensive run of melody, or of complicated harmony, is yet to be proved.

Jefferson's denigration of Wheatley seems aimed at the antislavery writers who since 1773 had cited her so frequently as proof positive of the equality of the African, and therefore as a reason to abolish slavery. Jefferson's critique of Phillis is unusually harsh:

> Misery is often the parent of the most affecting touches in poetry. Among the blacks is misery enough, God knows, but not poetry. Love is the peculiar oestrum of the poet. Their love is ardent, but it kindles the senses only, not the imagination. Religion, indeed, has produced a Phillis Whatley [sic]; but it could not produce a poet.

Jefferson was quite convinced that Wheatley's finer sentiments, such as her piety, are quite separate from the "love" needed to write poetry. What Jefferson meant is quite simple. He believed that Africans have human souls, they merely lack the intellectual endowments of other races. Like his contemporaries, he separated "what we would call intelligence from the capacity for religious experience." This division allows for both the religious conversion of slaves, as well as for the perpetuation of the principle of black inferiority. Guilt, as well as the growing evidence that blacks are indeed Homo sapiens, meant that Africans could no longer be regarded as brutes. So Jefferson accepted the souls and humanity of slaves, while still maintaining their inferiority. Phillis is, for Jefferson, an example of a product of religion, of mindless repetition and imitation, without being the product of intellect, of reflection. True art requires a sublime combination of feeling and reflection.

To illustrate more convincingly the inherent inferiority of the black mind, Jefferson compared the slaves in America to the ones of ancient Greece and Rome. After exposing the even greater duress under which the Roman slaves lived, Jefferson pointed to three famous, learned ones: "Epictetus, Terence, and Phaedrus, were slaves. But they were of the race of whites." From this fact, Jefferson drew his conclusion that it is not slavery, but an inherent mental inferiority, that has prevented the existence of Epictetus' black counterpart: "It is not [the blacks'] condition then, but nature which has produced the distinction." Sidestepping the full consequences such allegations of inferiority would have, Jefferson retreated behind the shelter of "suspicion": "I advance it, therefore, as a suspicion only, that the blacks, whether originally a distinct race, or made distinct by time and circumstances, are inferior to the whites in the endowments both of body and mind."

Unlike the American Indian, who is equal to the white in body, and whose mind is affected by external circumstances alone, the black is fundamentally different from the white. In reference to the Indians, Jefferson writes:

> To form a just estimate of their genius and mental powers, more facts are wanting, and a great allowance to be made for those

circumstances of their situation which call for a display find they are formed in mind as well as in body, on the same module with the Homo sapiens Europeans.

Jefferson recognized the capability for "improvement," especially mental improvement. He pointed to Europe, asking if the white person has not also shown, and needed time to show, progress in history:

> I may safely ask, how many good poets, how many able mathematicians, how many good inventors in arts and sciences, had Europe, north of the Alps, then produced? And it was sixteen centuries after [the Romans crossed the Alps] before a Newton could be formed.

One must make allowance, maintained Jefferson, for the fact that the Indian is not called on to display his intelligence in the same way as the European. The Indian displays his ca-

pabilities to the white person in the form of
war, in speeches, and in drawings:

> The Indians . . . will often carve figures on
> their pipes not destitute of design and
> merit. They will crayon out an animal, a
> plant, or a country, so as to prove the exis-
> tence of a germ in their minds which only
> wants cultivation.

Jefferson argued that the Indian's expres-
sions of reason, sentiment, and imagination
may be primitive, but they are potentially
equal to those of whites. While other races
and peoples advance and develop, the black
will be unable to do so. Unlike his thinking on
the Indian, Jefferson believed that there are
"real distinctions which nature has made,"
separating the blacks from the whites. Therefore, in the case of blacks, Jefferson disre-
garded the criteria by which he asserted
Indian mental equality: he does not advocate
making "a great allowance . . . for these cir-

cumstances of their situation which call for a display of particular talents only." For Thomas Jefferson, the black is a static element on the Great Chain of Being, and he will be left further down on the *scala naturae* as whites (and perhaps in sixteen centuries, the Indians) move up.

Jefferson reaches these conclusions, in some part, from his reading of Phillis Wheatley's poetry. Yes, he, concedes, she may very well have written these works, but they are derivative, imitative, devoid of that marriage of reason and transport that is, in his view, the peculiar oestrum of the poet. By shifting the terms of authenticity—from the very possibility of her authorship to the quality of her authorship—Jefferson indicted her for a failure of a higher form of authenticity. Having survived the tribunal of eighteen in 1772, Wheatley now finds her genuineness impugned by a larger authority, subjected to a higher test of originality and invention. And the complex rhetoric of authenticity would have a long, long afterlife.

To be sure, Jefferson's opinions generated scores of rebuttals: "reactions to Jefferson were immediate and they quickly proliferated," says William Robinson, writing on Wheatley two centuries after the publication of the *Notes*. "Indeed, much of the early Wheatley criticism is essentially rebuttal of Jeffersonian disdain." The most crucial aspect needing refutation was Jefferson's claim of the black's general inferiority to Europeans.

If Phillis Wheatley was the mother of African-American literature, there is a sense in which Thomas Jefferson can be thought of as its midwife. Blacks took on Jefferson's challenge immediately following the Revolution. As the historian Benjamin Quarles puts it, "Still unspent, the spirit of '76 found new outlets among blacks. The Revolutionary War as a black declaration of independence took on a power of its own, fueled by residual revolutionary rhetoric and sustained by the memory of fallen heroes and the cloud of the living black witness." Moreover, Jefferson's comments

about the role of their literature in any mean-
ingful assessment of the African-American's
civil rights became the strongest motivation
for blacks to create a body of literature that
would implicitly prove Jefferson wrong. This
is Wheatley's, and Jefferson's, curious legacy
in American literature.

It must be said that part of the fascination of
black intellectuals with Jefferson in the nineteenth century stemmed from rumors about his
paternity of Sally Hemings's children. Rather
than attempt to wade through complex DNA
data and genealogical records, I would rather
point to the tradition in black letters of naming
Jefferson as Sally's lover, which had its origins
in the nineteenth century. For example, at an
1860 meeting of the Pennsylvania Anti-Slavery
Society, a speaker described Jefferson as "a
good antislavery man." According to the
scholar Dorothy Sterling, he was interrupted
by shouts that "he sold his daughter!" The man
who took the floor was Robert Purvis, who had
inherited "a substantial fortune" from his white

father, a successful cotton broker, and had attended both Pittsfield and Amherst academies. He was a major figure in the abolitionist movement, becoming in 1839 the first president of the Vigilant Committee, which was in his words, "the first organized society of the Underground Railroad." He was well educated, articulate, and militant about black rights. He stood up and declared:

> Mr. Chairman, I am astonished at the audacity of the gentleman from Long Island in claiming Thomas Jefferson to be an antislavery man. Sir, Thomas Jefferson was a slaveholder and I hold all slaveholders to be tyrants and robbers. It is said that Thomas Jefferson sold his own daughter. This if true proves him to have been a scoundrel as well as a tyrant!
>
> Sir, I am free to confess that I have no veneration for the founders of this government, I do not share with others in their veneration for the "father of our country."

General Washington was a slaveholder, General Washington as President of the United States signed the fugitive Slave bill. General Washington tries, under the bill, to recover a poor woman flying through the perils and toils (thereby showing a truer courage than ever he did) that she might escape the yoke of slavery on his plantation.

When a man professing to be an Abolitionist has the—has the—Sir, I don't want to say audacity, but I can't think of any other word—to come here and hold a slaveholder as a good antislavery man, I forget all my resolutions to be guarded and speak with a vehemence which I afterwards regret.

Purvis must later have regretted calling Jefferson a "scoundrel" in his spoken remarks, because he deleted that word from the printed version.

The subject of Jefferson's black children assumed one of its first and most popular outlets in 1853, in William Wells Brown's novel *Clo-tel, or, The President's Daughter*. Published in London, as Wheatley's poem had been, it was the first novel to be published by an African American. Brown, the author of a slave narra-tive second only in sales and artistry to that of Frederick Douglass, was the tradition's first true man of letters, as Joyce Carol Oates re-cently pointed out. Brown published in a wide variety of genres, including poetry, travel writing, drama, and history, as well as fiction. *Clotel*'s action commences with the auction of Jefferson's mistress, as well as their two daughters, including Clotel herself. Clotel is later sold by the father of her child, escapes from a slave dealer only to be captured again (in the midst of Nat Turner's rebellion), is transferred to prison, where she escapes yet again—only to leap to her death in the Po-tomac rather than succumb to her captors.

To say that Brown was obsessed with the rumors of Jefferson's relation to Sally Hem-ings would be an understatement: Brown would revise and republish the story four times, once as a play in 1858, then, greatly revised, under new titles in 1860, 1864, and 1867, including a widely circulated serialized version. When Robert Purvis rose to speak about Jefferson at the anti-slavery meeting, it was Brown's version of the Jefferson legend that he had in mind. But Jefferson's relationship to Hemings and her children has been the stuff of the African-American oral tradition for two hundred years; even black historians addressed the subject before the recent controversy manifested itself in the works of Fawn Brodie and Annette Gordon-Reid. Indeed, I first encountered the story of Jefferson and Hemings in an old copy of *Ebony* magazine, dated 1954, and entitled "Thomas Jefferson's Negro Grandchildren," widely discussed in Mr. Coombie Carroll's barbershop in Keyser, West Virginia, even then.

Despite the titillating pleasure of oral reports of the Hemings-Jefferson liaison, it was Jefferson's *Notes* that preoccupied black and white abolitionists alike, containing as it did too many adamant allegations of black mental inferiority to be ignored. In fact, his statements acted as catalysts in sparking refutations of his opinions. The heated debate of black capacity and of the black's place in nature would continue well into the twentieth century.

Jefferson kept a commonplace book. It was edited and published by Gilbert Chinard in 1928. One of Jefferson's favorite citations from Horace, included therein, reads as follows:

> And, again, you cannot yourself bear to be in your company for an hour, you cannot employ your leisure aright, you shun yourself, a runaway vagabond, seeking now with wine, and now with sleep, to escape anxiety. In vain that black consort dogs and follows your flight.

If anxiety—figured here as "that black consort"—dogged Jefferson's steps relentlessly, then it can also be said that Mister Jefferson is the consort who has dogged African-American politics and letters. No Founding Father has been the subject of more speeches, essays, and books in the African-American tradition than Thomas Jefferson. No other figure has been more reviled yet, paradoxically, more revered; and no other figure has had a greater shaping impact upon both the discourse of black rights and the evolution of the African-American literary tradition than Thomas Jefferson.

The transformation of Jefferson's image into that of a motivator took its most curious and ironic form in the work of David Walker, whose *Appeal in Four Articles; Together with a Preamble, to the Coloured Citizens of the World, but in particular, and very expressly, to those of the United States of America* was published in Boston in 1829. It was, the scholar Peter P. Hinks tells us, "one of the nineteenth century's most incisive and vivid indictments of American racism and the insidious undermining it wrought on the black psyche."

Walker was never a slave; he was born to a free black woman in Wilmington, North Carolina, in 1796. In 1825 he moved to Boston, where he established a second-hand clothing business. Walker became the "principal agent" of *Freedom's Journal*, the nation's first black newspaper, first published in New York in 1827. We can get a sense of Walker's tone and content from the following passage:

> We, (coloured People of these United States), are the most degraded, wretched, and abject set of beings that ever lived since the world began . . . and the white Christians of America, who hold us in slavery, (or, more properly speaking, pretenders to Christianity), treat us more cruel and barbarous than any heathen nation did among people whom it had subjected.

Walker's relation to Jefferson was complex. Writing just three years after Jefferson's death—but forty-four years after Jefferson had written "Query XIV"—Walker walked a fine line between expressing his admiration for Jefferson's mind and the Declaration of Independence, in particular, yet refuting Jefferson's insinuations that blacks were not of the human family. Walker asked his readers if they realized "that Mr. Jefferson was one of as great a characters as ever lived among the whites?" And as such, Walker was determined to prove Mr. Jefferson wrong. Indeed, Jefferson's words, he continued, were not Jefferson's fault entirely, but were in part the fault of black people themselves. Refute the message "by your own actions," Walker argued, but don't shoot the messenger. Jefferson was wrong, but he was not the devil. No, Jefferson is "a man of such great learning, combined with such excellent natural parts." Indeed, he continued, Jefferson was sui generis: "a much greater philosopher the world has never afforded." It was precisely for that reason that his estimation carried such weight:

Now I ask you candidly, my suffering brethren in time, who are candidates for the eternal worlds, how could Mr. Jefferson but have given the world these remarks respecting us, when we are so submissive to them, and so much servile deceit prevail among ourselves—when we so *meanly* submit to their murderous lashes, to which neither the Indians nor any other people under Heaven would submit? No, they would die to a man, before they would suffer such things from men who are no better than themselves, and *perhaps not so good*. Yes, how can our friends but be embarrassed, as Mr. Jefferson says, by the question, "What further is to be done with these people?" For while they are working for our emancipation, we are, by our treachery, wickedness and deceit, working against ourselves and our children—helping ours, and the enemies of god, to keep us and our dear little children in their infernal chains of slavery!!!

Indeed, our friends cannot but relapse and join themselves "with those who are actuated by *sordid avarice only*!!!!" For my own part, I am glad Mr. Jefferson has advanced his positions for your sake; for you will either have to contradict or confirm him by your own actions, and not by what our friends have said or done for us; for those things are other men's labors, and do not satisfy the Americans, who are waiting for us to prove to them ourselves that we are men, before they will be willing to admit the fact; I pledge you my sacred word of honour. That honor, that Mr. Jefferson's remarks respecting us, have sunk deep into the hearts of millions of the whites, and never will be removed this side of eternity. For how can they, when we are confirming him every day, for our *groveling submissions* and *treachery*?

Not only did Walker's assessment of Jefferson's towering intellect shine through in this example, but Walker used both Jefferson's Declaration of Independence and the Constitution as the structural model for his pamphlet (his *Appeal* is in the form of "Articles"), citing the words of the Declaration as the model and rallying call for black freedom. "See your Declaration Americans!" he declared; "Do you understand your own language? Hear your language!" he exclaimed. Walker's appeal, ironically enough from the blackest and most militant man alive in 1829, is implicitly and explicitly a tribute in so many ways to Thomas Jefferson. When Nat Turner planned his famous revolt of 1831, a revolt many feel to have been inspired by Walker's *Appeal*, he chose July 4 as his ideal date to launch it, as a tribute to Jefferson's words.

I do not mean to imply that all black activists were willing to embrace Mr. Jefferson as the new architect of the tenets of their freedom struggle, or that the process was not a messy one, full of contradictions. William Hamilton wrestled out loud with this dilemma, in the year before Walker would publish the first edition of his *Appeal*. Hamilton was one of the dominant black figures in the antislavery movement from 1800 to his death in 1836.

Hamilton, in a speech in 1827, called Jefferson an ambidextrous philosopher "who can reason contrariwise," since he "first tells you that all men are created equal" and "next proves that one class of men are not equal to another." But in that same year, Hamilton himself exemplified a bit of this ambidexterity when, in a Fourth of July oration, he proposed that African Americans discontinue celebrating independence on that date. *Freedom's Journal*, in its July 11 and 18 issues, discusses the use of July 5, rather than the Fourth of July, as a sign of protest. Blacks such as William Wells Brown, Charles Lenox Redmond, and Charlotte Forten all spoke or wrote about the ironies of celebrating the Fourth of July in a nation where slavery remained legal. And no one was more vehement about this contradiction than was Frederick Douglass, whose

Fourth of July oration of 1852 was delivered in Rochester at the request of the Rochester Ladies' Anti-Slavery Society. "What, to the American slave, is your Fourth of July?" Douglass asks. "This Fourth of July is *yours* not *mine*. *You* may rejoice, *I* must mourn."

Nevertheless, despite his harsh indictment of the use of the Fourth as "a thin veil to cover up crimes which would disgrace a nation of savages," Douglass ends his speech by praising Jefferson's Declaration of Independence, "the great spirit it contains, and the genius of American Institutions."

James McCune Smith was another black thinker who notably and eloquently tried to show the error of Jefferson is his essay "On the Fourteenth Query of Thomas Jefferson's Notes on Virginia," published in the *Anglo-African Magazine* in August 1859. Calling Jefferson "the apostle of democracy," McCune Smith laid claim to the principles espoused by Jefferson in the Declaration of Independence, arguing that "we the people," on the eve of the

Civil War, applied equally to white and black precisely because the so-called blacks in Jefferson's day had become "colored people." "Let the American public but call men people," he write, "and those men . . . are already raised by the public voice into the dignity and privileges of citizenship."

The line of thinking articulated by Walker continued well into the 20th century: black authors accepted the premise that a group, a "race," had to demonstrate its equality through the creation of literature. When the historian David Levering Lewis aptly calls the Harlem Renaissance of the 1920s "art as civil rights," it is Jefferson who stands as the subtext for this formulation. Or listen to these words from James Weldon Johnson, written in 1922:

> A people may become great through many means, but there is only one measure by which its greatness is recognized and acknowledged. The final measure of the greatness of all peoples is the amount and

standard of the literature and art they have produced. No people that has produced great literature and art has ever been looked upon by the world as distinctly inferior.

In their efforts to prove Jefferson wrong, in other words, black writers created a body of literature, one with a prime political motive: to demonstrate black equality. Surely this is one of the oddest origins of a bellestric tradition in the history of world literature. Indeed, when Wole Soyinka received the Nobel Prize for Literature in 1986, a press release on behalf of the Nigerian government declared that—because of this prize—no longer could the world see Africans as distinctly inferior. The specter of Thomas Jefferson haunts even there, in Africa in 1986, as does the shadow of Phillis Wheatley.

Now, given all of the praise and attention that Wheatley received, given her unprecedented popularity and fame, one might be forgiven for thinking that Wheatley's career took off with the publication of her poems in 1773, and that she lived happily ever after. She did not. In the spring of 1774, the British occupied Boston. Susanna Wheatley died the same year, and when John Wheatley fled the city Phillis moved to Providence, where John Wheatley's daughter, Mary, and her husband lived. With the outbreak of war, in April of 1775, Phillis's prospects dimmed considerably. A number of the people who had signed the attestation were dead, and the others who had earlier supported her, both Tories and Patriots, were more concerned with winning the war than with the African prodigy. By late 1776, Wheatley had moved back to Boston. In 1778, she married a black man named John Peters. Peters was a small-time grocer and a sometime lawyer about whom very little is known—only that he successfully applied for the right to sell spirits in his store, and that a Wheatley relative remembered him as someone who affected the airs of a gentleman. Meanwhile, the poet continued her efforts to publish a second volume. In 1779, she advertised six times in the Boston *Evening Post & General Advertiser,* mentioning that she intended to dedicate the book to Benjamin Franklin. The advertisement failed to generate the necessary number of subscribers, and the book was never published.

Wheatley's freedom had enslaved her to a life of hardship. Peters abandoned her soon after she gave birth to their third child (the first two died in infancy). She placed her last advertisement in the September, 1784, issue of *The Boston Magazine* and died in December, at the age of thirty, poor and alone. Her baby died with her. Peters is thought to have sold the only copy of the second manuscript. Several poems from this manuscript have survived. A few years ago, one surfaced at Christie's and sold for nearly seventy thousand dollars, but the full manuscript has never been recovered.

And what happens to her literary legacy after she dies? Interwoven through Phillis

Wheatley's intriguing and troubling afterlife is a larger parable about the politics of authenticity. For, as I've said, those rituals of validation scarcely died with Phillis Wheatley; on the contrary, they would become a central theme in the abolitionist era, where the publication of the slave narratives by and large also depended on letters of authentication that testified to the veracity and capacities of the ex-slave author who had written this work "by himself" or "by herself."

One might be forgiven, too, for imagining that Phillis Wheatley would be among the most venerated names among black Americans today, as celebrated as Frederick Douglass, Rosa Parks, or Dr. Martin Luther King, Jr. It was probably true that, as one writer claimed several years ago, "historically throughout black America, more YMCAs, schools, dormitories and libraries have been named for Phillis Wheatley than for any other black woman." And, indeed, I can testify to the presence before 1955 of the Phillis Wheatley Elementary School in Ridgeley, West Virginia, a couple of hours up the Potomac, near Piedmont, where I grew up—though it took until college for me to learn just who Miss Wheatley was.

That Phillis Wheatley is not a household word within the black community is owing largely to one poem that she wrote, an eight-line poem entitled "On Being Brought from Africa to America." The poem was written in 1768, just seven years after Phillis was purchased by Susanna Wheatley. Phillis was about fourteen years old.

The eight-line poem reads as follows:

'Twas mercy brought me from my *Pagan*
    land,
Taught my benighted soul to understand
That there's a God, that there's a *Saviour*
    too:
Once I redemption neither sought nor
    knew.
Some view our sable race with scornful eye,

"Their coulour is a diabolic die,"
Remember, *Christians*, *Negros*, black as *Cain*,
May be refin'd, and join th' angelic train.

This, it can be safely said, has been the most reviled poem in African-American literature. To speak in such glowing terms about the "mercy" manifested by the slave trade was not exactly going to endear Miss Wheatley to black power advocates in the 1960s. No Angela Davis she! But as scholars such as William Robinson, Julian Mason, John Shields, and Vincent Carretta point out, her political detractors ignore the fact that Wheatley elsewhere in her poems complained bitterly about the human costs of the slave trade, as in this example from her famous poem, "To the Right Honourable William, Earl of Dartmouth."

Should you, my lord, while you peruse my
song,

Wonder from whence my love of *Freedom*
    sprung,
Whence flow these wishes for the common
    good,
By feeling hearts alone best understood,
I, young in life, by seeming cruel fate
Was snatch'd from *Afric's* fancy'd happy
    seat:
What pangs excruciating must molest,
What sorrows labour in my parent's breasts
Steel'd was that soul and by no misery
    mov'd
That from a father seiz'd his babe belov'd:
Such, such my case. And can I then but pray
Others may never feel tyrannic sway?

And there is Wheatley's letter to the Reverend Samson Occom, "a converted Mohegan
Indian Christian Minister" who was the eighteenth century's most distinguished graduate
from Moor's Charity Indian School of
Lebanon, Connecticut, which would relocate

in 1770 to Hanover, New Hampshire, where it would be renamed after the Earl of Dartmouth (and its student body broadened, against many protests, to include whites). The letter was published several months after her manumission. It appeared in *The Connecticut Gazette* on March 11, 1774, and reads, in part:

> In every human Breast, God has implanted a Principle, which we call Love of Freedom; it is impatient of Oppression, and pants for Deliverance; and by the Leave of our modern Egyptians I will assert, that the same Principle lives in us. God grant Deliverance in his own Way and Time, and grant his honour upon all those whose Avarice impels them to countenance and help the Calamities of their fellow Creatures. This I desire not for their Hurt, but to convince them of the strange Absurdity of their Conduct whose Words and actions are so diametrically opposite. How well the Cry for Liberty, and the reverse Disposition for the exercise

of oppressive Power over others agree,—I
humbly think it does not require the Pene-
tration of a Philosopher to determine.

Despite sentiments such as these, the fact
that Wheatley's short poem has been so
widely anthologized in this century has
made her something of a pariah in black political and critical circles, especially in the
militant 1960s, where critics had a field day
mocking her life and her works (most of
which they had not read).

Until the emergence of Frederick Douglass, Wheatley was commonly used as an
icon of black intellectual perfectibility by the
abolitionist movement. Even in the late 1840s
and 50s works such as Wilson Armistead's *A
Tribute for the Negro* (1848) and Martin R. Delany's *The Condition, Elevation, Emigration,
and Destiny of the Colored People of the United
States, Politically Considered* (1852) were ful-
some in their praise of Wheatley and her poetry. We can trace the anti-Wheatley tendency

at least to 1887, when Edward Wilmot Blyden, one of the fathers of black nationalism, wrote about her contemptuously, and the tone was set for the century to come. James Weldon Johnson, writing in 1922, complained that "one looks in vain for some outburst or even complaint against the bondage of her people, for some agonizing cry about her native land," finding instead a "smug contentment at her escape therefrom."

But what really laid her low was ultimately a cultural critique of her work—less what she said than the way she said it.

Wallace Thurman, writing in 1928, calls her "a third-rate imitation" of Alexander Pope: "Phillis in her day was a museum figure who would have caused more of a sensation if some contemporary Barnum had exploited her."

Vernon Loggins, in his masterful history of Negro literature, published in 1930, echoes Jefferson when he says that Wheatley's poetry reflects "her instinct for hearing the music of words" rather than understanding their meaning, "an instinct," he concludes, "which is racial." She lacks the capacity to reflect, to think. For Loggins, as E. Lynn Matson puts it, Wheatley is "a clever imitator, nothing more."

By the mid-sixties, criticism of Wheatley rose to a high pitch of disdain. Amiri Baraka, a founder of the Black Arts Movement, wrote in 1962 that Wheatley's "pleasant imitations of eighteenth-century English poetry are far and, finally, ludicrous departures from the huge black voices that splintered southern nights with their *hollers*, *chants*, *arwhoolies*, and *ballits*." For him, of course, these chants represent the authentic spirit of black creativity. Seymour Gross, writing in 1966 in "Images of the Negro in American Literature," argued that "this Negro poetess so well fits the Uncle Tom syndrome. . . . She is pious, grateful, retiring, and civil." As William Robinson reports, other critics called Wheatley "an early Boston Aunt Jemima," "a colonial handkerchief head," and "utterly irrelevant to the identification and liberation of the black man." She was finally, "oblivious to the lot of her fellow blacks."

Stephen Henderson, writing in *The Militant Black Writer*, (1969), argues that "it is no wonder that many black people have rejected Phillis Wheatley," because her work reflects "the old self-hatred that one hears in the Dozens and in the blues. It is, frankly," he concludes, "the nigger component of the Black Experience." Dudley Randall wrote in that same year that "whatever references she made to her African heritage were derogatory, reflecting her status as a favored house slave and a curiosity." In 1971 Nathan Higgins wrote that Wheatley's voice was that of "a feeble Alexander Pope rather than that of an African prince."

Addison Gayle, Jr., a major black aesthetic critic, wrote in *The Way of the World* (1975) that Wheatley was the first black writer "to accept the images and symbols of degradation passed down from the South's most intellectual lights and the first to speak from a sensibility finely tuned by close ap-proximation to [her] oppressors." Wheatley, in sum, "had surrendered the right to self-definition to others."

And the assaults continued, the critical ar-rows arriving in waves. This once most-revered figure in black letters would, in the sixties, become the most reviled figure. Ange-lene Jamison argued in 1974 that Wheatley and her poetry were "too white," a sentiment that Ezekiel Mphalele echoed two years later when he indicted her for having "a white mind," and said he felt "too embarrassed even to mention her in passing" in a study of black literature. Similarly, Eleanor Smith main-tained that Wheatley was "taught by whites to think," thus she had "a white mind" and "white orientations." Here we're given Phillis Wheatley as Uncle Tom's mother.

As the scholar Russell Reising notes, this trend from the Black Arts Movement of the sixties has unduly informed criticism of Wheatley through the eighties:

Angelene Jamison takes a pedagogical and political tack similar to Smith's when she argues that Wheatley's poetry "embraces white attitudes and values, and it characterizes Phillis as a typical Euro-American poetess." She was detached from her people and her poetry could never be used as an expression of black thought (409). While Jamison grants that Wheatley should not be ignored because of her accommodationist stance, she asserts that "teaching Phillis Wheatley from a black perspective shows that she was simply an eighteenth-century poet who supported, praised, and imitated those who enslaved her and her people" (416). Other critics echo these sentiments when they suggest that Wheatley "leaves the reader of her poems only slightly aware of her being a Negro and a slave" (Mason xxv), that her poems "serve as one measure of how far removed from the reality of her blackness Phillis had become" (Collins 149), and that "the Wheatleys had adopted her, but she had adopted their terrific New England conscience" (Redding 9). While progressively more modulated, similar sentiments inform Wheatley criticism of the 1980s. Alice Walker, for example, expresses a blend of compassion for and amazement at the "sickly little black girl," but nonetheless regards her poetry as "stiff, struggling, ambivalent," and "bewildered" (237). In 1986, June Jordan, while sensing the political and ontological ambivalence experienced by Wheatley and while grasping the explicit resistance to tyranny in a number of Wheatley's poems, still assumes that much of what happens in Wheatley's verse can be attributed to "regular kinds of iniquitous nonsense found in white literature, the literature that Phillis Wheatley assimilated, with no choice in the matter" (255). Kenneth Silverman's cultural history of the American Revolution assumes this same trajectory, agreeing that Wheatley's work is a simple paean to white, cultural hegemony (217).

Although the critical reception to Wheatley and her poetry by contemporary African-American critics has been largely negative, there has, of course, always been a counter-narrative, but in a distinctly minor key. As Kenneth W. Warren notes, in 1892, Anna Julia Cooper praised Wheatley in her collection of essays *A Voice from the South*; in the 1920s her works appeared in anthologies of African-American poetry; W. E. B. Du Bois complimented her in an essay published in 1941; and in 1973, Margaret Walker's famous bicentennial celebration of Wheatley's poems at Jackson State College was attended by leading African-American writers and scholars. Nonetheless, the overwhelming tendency in Wheatley criticism has been to upbraid her for "not being black enough."

And unfortunately, the examples of recent criticism that Reising supplies could be multiplied. It's clear enough what we're witnessing. The Jeffersonian critique has been recuperated and recycled by successive generations of black writers and critics. Too black to be taken seriously by white critics in the eighteenth century, Wheatley was now considered too white to interest black critics in the twentieth. Precisely the sort of mastery of the literary craft and themes that led to her vindication before the Boston town-hall tribunal was now summoned as proof that she was, culturally, an impostor. Phillis Wheatley, having been pain-stakingly authenticated in her own time, now stands as a symbol of falsity, artificiality, of spiritless and rote convention. As new cultural vanguards sought to police and patrol the boundaries of black art, Wheatley's glorious carriage would become a tumbril.

Phillis Wheatley, who had once been cast as the great paragon of Negro achievement, was now given a new role: race traitor.

I am not the only scholar who has wished the teenage poet had found a more veiled way to express her gratitude to Susanna Wheatley for saving her from a worse form of slavery and for expressing her genuine joy at her full embrace of Christianity. But it's striking that Jefferson and Amiri Baraka, two figures in American letters who would agree on little else, could agree on the terms of their indictment of Phillis Wheatley.

For Wheatley's critics, her sacrifices, her courage, her humiliations, her trials would never be enough. And so we have come full circle: the sort of racist suspicions and anxieties that attended Wheatley's writing are now directed at forms of black expression that seem to fail of a new sort of authenticity, as determined by a yardstick of cultural affirmation. Today the question has become "Who is black enough?" The critics of the Black Arts Movement and after were convening their own interrogation squad, and they were a rather more hostile group than met that day in 1772. We can almost imagine Wheatley being frog-marched through another hall in the nineteen-sixties or seventies, surrounded by dashiki-clad, flowering figures of "the Revolution": "What is Ogun's relation to Esu?" "Who are the sixteen principal deities in the Yoruba pantheon of Gods?" "Santeria derived from which African culture?" And finally: "Where you gonna be when the revolution comes, *sista*?"

And this has not merely turned out to be a sixties phenomenon. Those haunting questions of identity linger with us still, much to the devastation of inner-city youth. I read with dismay the results of a poll published a few years ago. The charge of "acting white" was applied to speaking standard English, getting straight A's, or even visiting the Smithsonian! Think about it: we have moved from a situation where Phillis Wheatley's acts of literacy could be used to demonstrate our people's inherent humanity and their inalienable right to freedom, to a situation where acts of literacy are stigmatized somehow as acts of racial betrayal. Phillis Wheatley, so proud to the end of her hard-won attainments, would weep. So would Douglass; so would Du Bois. In reviving the ideology of "authenticity"— especially in a Hip Hop world where too many of our children think it's easier to become Michael Jordan than Vernon Jordan— we have ourselves reforged the manacles of an earlier, admittedly racist era.

And, even now, so the imperative remains: to cast aside the mine-and-thine rhetoric of cultural ownership. For cultures can no more be owned than people can. As W. E. B. Du Bois put it so poignantly:

I sit with Shakespeare and he winces not. Across the color line I move arm and arm with Balzac and Dumas, where smiling men and welcoming women glide in gilded halls. From out the caves of evening that swing between the strong-limbed earth and the tracery of the stars, I summon Aristotle and Aurelius and what soul I will, and they come all graciously with no

scorn nor condescension. So, wed with
Truth, I dwell above the veil.

This is the vision that we must embrace, as
full and equal citizens of the republic of letters, a republic whose citizenry must always
embrace both Phillis Wheatley and Thomas
Jefferson.

Frederick Douglass recognized this
clearly; in a speech delivered in 1863, at the
height of the Civil War, Douglass argued
that his contemporaries in the Confederacy
selectively cited Jefferson's pro-slavery writings when convenient, ignoring the rest. For
Douglass, black Americans were the true patriots, because they fully embraced Jeffersonian democracy; they were the most
Jeffersonian Americans of all, allowing us to
witness a new way to appreciate the miracle
that is America. Here was Jefferson, whom
Douglass called "the sage of the Old Domin-
ion," cast as the patron saint of the black
freedom struggle.

If Frederick Douglass could recuperate and champion Thomas Jefferson, during the Civil War of all times, is it possible for us to do the same for a modest young poet named Phillis Wheatley? What's required is only that we recognize that there are no "white minds" or "black minds": there are only minds, and yes, they are, as that slogan has it, a terrible thing to waste. What would happen if we ceased to stereotype Wheatley but, instead, read her, read her with all the resourcefulness that she herself brought to her craft? I can already hear the skeptics: that's all well and good, they'll say, but how is it possible to read Wheatley's "On Being Brought from Africa to America?" But, of course, there are few things that cannot be redeemed by those of charitable inclination. And just a few days after a recent Fourth of July, I received a fax from a man named Walter Grigo, sent from a public fax machine in Madison, Connecticut.

Mr. Grigo—a freelance writer—had evidently become fascinated with anagrams, and

wished to alert me to quite a stunning anagram indeed. "On Being Brought from Africa
to America," this eight-line poem, was, in its
entirety, an anagram, he pointed out. If you
simply rearranged the letters, you got the following plea:

> Hail, Brethren in Christ! Have ye
> Forgotten God's word? Scriptures teach
> Us that bondage is wrong. His own greedy
> Kin sold Joseph into slavery. "Is there
> No balm in Gilead?" God made us all.
> Aren't African men born to be free? So
> Am I. Ye commit so brute a crime
> On us. But we can change thy attitude.
> America, manumit our race. I thank the
> Lord.

It is indeed the case that every letter in
Wheatley's poem can be rearranged to pro-
duce an entirely new work, one with the re-
verse meaning of the apologetic and infamous

original. Grigo adds that the title of the poem, "On Being Brought from Africa to America," can be rearranged to read "Bitter, Go I, Ebon Human Cargo, From Africa." Moreover, he continues, the five italicized words—Pagan, Savior, Christians, Negroes, Cain—are an anagram of "grasp a great vision: no races in chains." "Could it be that Phillis Wheatley was this devious?" Mr. Grigo asked me. And it is fun to think that the most scorned poem in the tradition, all this time, was a secret, coded love letter to freedom, hiding before our very eyes. I don't claim that this stratagem was the result of design, but we're free to find significance, intended or not, where we un-cover it.

And so we're reminded of our task, as readers: to learn to read Wheatley anew, un-blinkered by the anxieties of her time and ours. That's the only way to let Phillis Wheatley take the stand. The challenge isn't to read white, or read black; it is to read. If Wheatley stood for anything, it was the creed

that culture was, could be, the equal possession of all humanity. It was a lesson she was
swift to teach, and that we have been slow to
learn. But the learning has begun. Almost
two and a half centuries after a schooner
brought this African child to our shores, we
can finally say: Welcome home, Phillis; welcome home.

Bibliography

Editions of the Writings of Phillis Wheatley

Carretta, Vincent, ed. *Phillis Wheatley: Complete Writings*. New York: Penguin Books, 2001.

Mason, Julian D., Jr., ed. *The Poems of Phillis Wheatley: Revised and Enlarged Edition*. Chapel Hill: University of North Carolina Press, 1989.

Robinson, William H. *Phillis Wheatley and Her Writings*. New York: Garland, 1984.

Shields, John C., ed. *The Collected Works of Phillis Wheatley*. New York: Oxford University Press, 1988.

Bibliography

Nine biographies of Boston's eighteen "most respectable characters" can be found in the
American National Biography, 24 vols. (New
York: Oxford University Press, 1999), including the following:

Calhoon, Robert M. "Andrew Oliver." Vol. 16,
684–86;

———. "Thomas Hutchinson." Vol. 11, 597–600;

Fowler, William M., Jr. "John Hancock." Vol. 9,
968–70;

Kershaw, Gordon E. "James Bowdoin." Vol. 3,
272–74;

Lippy, Charles A. "Charles Chauncy." Vol. 4,
753–55;

Lowance, Mason I. "Samuel Mather." Vol. 14, 693;

McCarl, Mary Rhinelander. "Mather Byles." Vol.
4, 130–31;

Mills, Frederick V., Sr. "Samuel Cooper." Vol. 5,
456–57;

Robinson, David M. "Joseph Green." Vol. 9,
499–500.

In addition, biographical data on John Erving and
James Pitts can be found in the *ANB* entry for

James Bowdoin; Erving is Bowdoin's father-in-law and Pitts is his brother-in-law. Information about Thomas Hubbard, Ebenezer Pemberton, and John Moorhead is found in William H. Robinson's *Phillis Wheatley and Her Writings* (New York: Garland, 1984).

Secondary Sources on Phillis Wheatley and Thomas Jefferson

Akers, Charles. "'Our Modern Egyptians': Phillis Wheatley and the Whig Campaign Against Slavery in Revolutionary Boston." *Journal of Negro History* 60 (1975).

Applegate, Ann. "Phillis Wheatley: Her Critics and Her Contribution." *Negro American Literature Forum* 9 (1975): 123–26.

Armistead, Wilson. *A Tribute for the Negro: Being a Vindication of the Moral, Intellectual, and Religious Capabilities of the Coloured Portion of Mankind, with Particular Reference to the African Race*. Westport, CT: Negro Universities Press, 1970.

Bibliography

Bacon, Martha. *Puritan Promenade*. Boston: Houghton Mifflin, 1964.

Baker, Houston A., Jr. *The Journey Back: Issues in Black Literature and Criticism*. Chicago: University of Chicago Press, 1980.

———. *Workings of the Spirit: The Poetics of Afro-American Women's Writing*. Chicago: University of Chicago Press, 1991.

Baym, Max I. *A History of Literary Aesthetics in America*. New York: Frederick Ungar, 1973.

Beard, Eva. "A Friend in High Places: Thomas Jefferson." *The Crisis* 54.4 (April 1947): 111–24.

Bennett, Paula. "Phillis Wheatley's Vocation and the Paradox of the 'Afric Muse.'" *PMLA* 113.1 (1998): 64–76.

Berman, Eleanor Davidson. *Thomas Jefferson Among the Arts: An Essay in Early American Esthetics*. New York: Philosophical Library, 1947.

Bly, Antonio T. "Wheatley's 'On the Affray in King Street.'" *Explicator* 56.4 (1998): 177–80.

_____. "Wheatley's 'On the Death of a Young Lady of Five Years of Age.'" *Explicator* 58.1 (1999): 10–13.

_____. "Wheatley's 'To the University of Cambridge in New-England.'" *Explicator* 55.4 (1997): 205–8.

Blyden, Edward Wilmot. *Christianity, Islam, and the Negro Race*. London: W. B. Whittington, 1887.

Boulton, Alexander O. "The American Paradox: Jeffersonian Equality and Racial Science." *American Quarterly* 47.3 (September 1995): 467–93.

Brawley, Benjamin Griffith. *Negro Builders and Heroes*. Chapel Hill: University of North Carolina Press, 1937.

Brawley, Benjamin Griffith, ed. *Early Negro American Writers: Selections with Biographical and Critical Introductions*. Chapel Hill: University of North Carolina Press, 1935. 31–55.

Bridenbaugh, Carl. "The First Published Poems of Phillis Wheatley." *New England Quarterly* 42 (December 1969): 583–84.

Brodie, Fawn M. *Thomas Jefferson: An Intimate History*. New York: Bantam Books, 1975.

Brown, William Wells. *Clotel; or, the President's Daughter: A Narrative of Slave Life in the United States*. London: n.p., 1853.

Burke, Helen. "Problematizing American Dissent: The Subject of Phillis Wheatley." *Cohesion and Dissent in America*. Eds. Carol Colatrella and Joseph Alkana. Albany: State University of New York Press, 1994. 193–209.

_____. "The Rhetoric and Politics of Marginality: The Subject of Phillis Wheatley." *Tulsa Studies in Women's Literature* 10.1 (Spring 1991): 31–45.

Carretta, Vincent. "Phillis Wheatley, the Mansfield Decision of 1772, and the Choice of Identity." *Early America Re-Explored: New Readings in Colonial, Early National, and Antebellum Culture*. Eds. and introd. Klaus H.

Schmidt and Fritz Fleischmann. New York: Peter Lang, 2000. 201–23.

Carretta, Vincent, and Philip Gould, eds. *Genius in Bondage: Literature of the Early Black Atlantic*. Lexington: University of Kentucky Press, 2001.

Chase, Eugene P. trans. and ed. *Our Revolutionary Forefathers; the Letters of Francois, Marquis de Barbé-Marbois during His Residence in the United States as Secretary of the French Legation, 1779–1785*. New York: Duffield, 1929.

Chinard, Gilbert. *The Literary Bible of Thomas Jefferson*. Baltimore: Johns Hopkins University Press, 1928.

Choucair, Mona M. "Phillis Wheatley (1754–1784)." *African American Authors, 1745–1945: A Bio-Bibliographical Critical Sourcebook*. Ed. and pref. Emmanuel S. Nelson. Wesport, CT: Greenwood, 2000. 463–68.

Cima, Gay Gibson. "Black and Unmarked: Phillis Wheatley, Mercy Otis Warren, and the Limits of Strategic Anonymity." *Theatre Journal* 52.4 (December 2000): 465–95.

Collins, Terence. "Phillis Wheatley: The Dark Side of the Poetry." *Phylon: The Atlanta University Review of Race and Culture* 36 (1975): 78–88.

Connor, Kimberly Rae. *Conversions and Vision in the Writings of African-American Women*. Knoxville: University of Tennessee Press, 1994.

Cook, Mercer, and Stephen E. Henderson. *The Militant Black Writer in Africa and the United States*. Madison: University of Wisconsin Press, 1969.

Daly, Robert. "Powers of Humility and the Presence of Readers in Anne Bradstreet and Phillis Wheatley." *Puritanism in America: The Seventeenth through the Nineteenth Centuries*. Ed. Michael Schuldiner. Lewiston, NY: Mellen, 1993. 1–24.

Davis, David Brion. *The Problem of Slavery in the Age of Revolution, 1770–1823*. New York: Oxford University Press, 1998.

_____. *The Problem of Slavery in Western Thought*. Ithaca: Cornell University Press, 1966.

Davis, Gwenn, and Beverly A. Joyce, eds. *Poetry by Women to 1900: A Bibliography of American and British Writers*. Toronto: University of Toronto Press, 1991.

Deane, Charles, ed. *Letters of Phillis Wheatly [sic], the Negro-Slave Poet of Boston*. Boston: J. Wilson and Son, 1864.

Delany, Martin R. *The Condition, Elevation, Emigration, and Destiny of the Colored People of the United States*. Rpt. ed. Introd. Benjamin Quarles. Salem, NH: Ayer Company, 1988.

Douglass, Frederick. "The Proclamation and a Negro Army." Ed. Philip S. Foner. *The Life and Writings of Frederick Douglass*. Vol. 3. New York: International Publishers, 1952. 321–37.

Du Bois, W. E. B. *The Souls of Black Folk*. Introd. Donald B. Gibson. New York: Penguin Books, 1989.

Ellison, Julie. "The Politics of Fancy in the Age of Sensibility." *Re-Visioning Romanticism: British Women Writers, 1776–1837*. Eds. Carol Shiner Wilson and Jean Haefner. Philadelphia: University of Pennsylvania Press, 1994. 228–55.

Erkkila, Betsy. "Phillis Wheatley and the Black American Revolution." *A Mixed Race: Ethnicity in Early America*. Ed. Frank Shuffleton. New York: Oxford University Press, 1993. 225–40.

_____. "Revolutionary Women." *Tulsa Studies in Women's Literature* 6.2 (1987): 189–223.

Felker, Christopher. "'The Tongues of the Learned Are Insufficient': Phillis Wheatley, Publishing Objectives, and Personal Liberty." *Texts and Textuality: Textual Instability, Theory, and Interpretation*. Ed. and introd. Philip Cohen. New York: Garland, 1997. 81–119.

Flanzbaum, Hilene. "Unprecedented Liberties: Re-Reading Phillis Wheatley." *MELUS: The Journal of the Society for the Study of Multi-Ethnic Literature of the United States* 18.3 (1993): 71–81.

Foster, Frances Smith. *Written by Herself: Literary Production by African-American Women, 1746–1892*. Bloomington: Indiana University Press, 1993.

Garnet, Henry Highland. "Address to the Slaves." *The Black Abolitionist Papers*. Ed. C. Peter Ripley. Vol. 3. Chapel Hill: University of North Carolina Press, 1991. 403–12.

Gates, Henry Louis, Jr. *Figures in Black: Words, Signs, and the "Racial" Self*. New York: Oxford University Press, 1987.

_____. "From Wheatley to Douglass: The Politics of Displacement." *Frederick Douglass: New Literary and Historical Essays*. Ed. Eric J. Sundquist. Cambridge: Cambridge University Press, 1991. 47–65.

_____. "Phillis Wheatley and the Nature of the Negro." Robinson, *Critical Essays* 215–33.

_____. "Phillis Wheatley on Trial." *The New Yorker* 20 January 2003: 82–88.

_____. *The Signifying Monkey: A Theory of African-American Literary Criticism*. New York: Oxford University Press, 1988.

Gayle, Addison, Jr. *Black Expression: Essays by and about Black Americans in the Creative Arts*. New York: Weybright and Talley, 1969.

_____. *The Way of the New World: The Black Novel in America*. Garden City, NY: Anchor Press, 1975.

Gordon-Reed, Annette. "Engaging Jefferson: Blacks and the Founding Father." *William and Mary Quarterly* 3rd ser. LVII.1 (January 2000): 171–82.

_____. *Thomas Jefferson and Sally Hemings: An American Controversy*. Charlottesville: University of Virginia Press, 1997.

Graham, Shirley. *The Story of Phillis Wheatley*. New York: J. Messner, 1949.

Greenberg, Kenneth S., ed. and introd. *The Confessions of Nat Turner and Related Documents*. Boston: Bedford Books of St. Martin's Press, 1996.

Grimsted, David. "Anglo-American Racism and Phillis Wheatley's 'Sable Veil,' 'Length'ned Chain,' and 'Knitted Heart.'" *Women in the Age of the American Revolution*. Eds. Ronald Hoffman and Peter J. Albert. Charlottesville: University of Virginia Press, 1989. 338–44.

Hamilton, William. "An Oration Delivered in the African Zion Church, on the Fourth of July, 1827, in Commemoration of the Abolition of Domestic Slavery in This State" (New York: Gray and Bunce, 1827). Porter 96–104.

Harris, Sharon M. "Early Women's Texts." *Teaching the Literatures of Early America*. Ed. Carla Mulford. New York: Modern Language Association of America, 1999. 48–62.

_____. "Whose Past Is It? Women Writers in Early America." *Early American Literature* 30.2 (1995): 175–81.

Hayden, Lucy K. "Classical Tidings from the Afric Muse: Phillis Wheatley's Use of Greek and Roman Mythology." *CLA Journal* 35.4 (1992): 432–47.

Heartman, Charles F. *Phillis Wheatley: A Critical Attempt and a Bibliography of Her Writings*. New York: Printed for the author, 1915.

Herron, Carolivia. "Early African American Poetry." *The Columbia History of American Poetry*. Eds. Jay Parini and Brett C. Miller. New

York: Columbia University Press, 1993. 16–32.

————. "Milton and Afro-American Literature." *Re-Membering Milton: Essays on the Texts and Traditions*. Eds. Mary Nyquist and Margaret W. Ferguson. New York: Methuen, 1987. 278–300.

Hinks, Peter P., ed. and introd. *David Walker's Appeal to the Coloured Citizens of the World*. University Park: Pennsylvania State University Press, 2000.

————. *To Awaken My Afflicted Brethren: David Walker and the Problem of Antebellum Slave Resistance*. University Park: Pennsylvania State University Press, 1997.

Holloway, Karla F. C. "The Body Politic." *Subjects and Citizens: Nation, Race, and Gender from Oroonoko to Anita Hill*. Eds. Michael Moon and Cathy N. Davidson. Durham: Duke University Press, 1995. 481–95.

Holly, Joseph C. "American Slavery—Its Effects upon the Rights and Interests of the North." *The Black Abolitionist Papers*. Vol. 4. Chapel

Hill: University of North Carolina Press, 1991. 18–26.

Huggins, Nathan. *Harlem Renaissance*. New York: Oxford University Press, 1971.

Hume, David. "Of National Characters." *The Philosophical Works of David Hume*. Vol. 111. Boston: Little, Brown and Company, 1854. 217–36.

Isani, Mukhtar Ali. "The British Reception of Wheatley's Poems on Various Subjects." *Journal of Negro History* 66 (Summer 1981): 144–49.

_____. "Early Versions of Some Works of Phillis Wheatley." *Early American Literature* 14 (1979): 149–55.

_____. "'An Elegy on Leaving —': A New Poem by Phillis Wheatley." *American Literature* 58.4 (December 1986): 609–13.

_____. "The First Proposed Edition of Poems on Various Subjects and the Phillis Wheatley Canon." *American Literature* 49 (1977): 97–103.

_____. "'Gambia on My Soul': Africa and the African in the Writings of Phillis Wheatley."

MELUS: The Journal of the Society for the Study of Multi-Ethnic Literature of the United States 6 (1979): 64–72.

_____. "The Methodist Connection: New Variants on Some Phillis Wheatley Poems." *Early American Literature* 22.1 (Spring 1987): 108–13.

_____. "'On the Death of General Wooster': An Unpublished Poem by Phillis Wheatley." *Modern Philology* 77 (1980): 306–9.

_____. "Phillis Wheatley and the Elegiac Mode." Robinson, *Critical Essays* 208–14.

_____. "Phillis Wheatley in London: An Unpublished Letter to David Wooster." *American Literature* 51 (1979): 255–60.

Jackson, Sarah Dunlap. "Letters of Phillis Wheatley and Susanna Wheatley." *Journal of Negro History* 58 (April 1972): 212.

Jamison, Angelene. "Analysis of Selected Poetry of Phillis Wheatley." *Journal of Negro Education* 43.3 (1974): 408–16.

Jefferson, Thomas. *Notes on the State of Virginia.* Ed. and introd. Frank Shuffleton. New York: Penguin Books, 1999.

_____. "Thoughts on English Prosody." *The Writings of Thomas Jefferson*. Vol. XVIII. Eds. Andrew A. Lipscomb and Albert Ellery Bergh. Washington, D.C.: Thomas Jefferson Memorial Association of the United States, 1907. 414–51.

Jennings, Regina. "African Sun Imagery in the Poetry of Phillis Wheatley." *Pennsylvania English* 22.1–2 (Fall-Spring 2000): 68–76.

Johnson, Barbara E. "Euphemism, Understatement, and the Passive Voice: A Genealogy of Afro-American Poetry." *Reading Black, Reading Feminist: A Critical Anthology*. Ed. Henry Louis Gates, Jr. New York: Meridian, 1990. 204–11.

Johnson, James Weldon, ed. *The Book of American Negro Poetry*. New York: Harcourt, Brace and Company, 1931.

Jones, LeRoi. "The Myth of a 'Negro Literature.'" Gayle, *Black Expression* 190–91.

Jordan, June. "The Difficult Miracle of Black Poetry in America; Or, Something Like a Sonnet for Phillis Wheatley." *Massachusetts Review* 27.2 (Summer 1986): 252–62.

Jordan, Winthrop. *White Over Black: American Racial Attitudes to the Negro, 1550–1812*. Chapel Hill: University of North Carolina Press, 1967.

Kallen, Horace M. "The Arts and Thomas Jefferson." *Ethics* LIII (July 1943): 269–83.

Kant, Immanuel. *Observations on the Feeling of the Beautiful and the Sublime*. Trans. T. Goldthwait. Berkeley: University of California Press, 1981.

Kaplan, Lawrence S. *Jefferson and France: An Essay on Politics and Political Ideas*. New Haven, CT: Yale University Press, 1967.

Kaplan, Sidney. "Phillis Wheatley." *The Black Presence in the Era of the American Revolution, 1770–1800*. Greenwich, CT: New York Graphic Society, 1973. 150–70.

Kendrick, Robert. "Other Questions: Phillis Wheatley and the Ethics of Interpretation." *Cultural Critique* 38 (1998): 39–64.

_____. "Re-Membering America: Phillis Wheatley's Intertextual Epic." *African American Review* 30.1 (1996): 71–88.

_____. "Snatching a Laurel, Wearing a Mask: Phillis Wheatley's Literary Nationalism and the Problem of Style." *Style* 27.2 (1993): 222–51.

Kimball, Fiske. "Jefferson and the Arts." *Proceedings of the American Philosophical Society* 87 (July 1943): 223–34.

Klinkowitz, Jerome. "Early Writers: Jupiter Hammon, Phillis Wheatley, and Benjamin Banneker." *Black American Writers: Bibliographical Essays*. Eds. M. Thomas Inge, Maurice Duke, Jackson R. Bryer. 2 vols. New York: St. Martin's Press, 1978. 1–20.

Kuncio, Robert C. "Some Unpublished Poems of Phillis Wheatley." *New England Quarterly* 43 (June 1970): 287–97.

Lapsansky, Philip. "'Deism': An Unpublished Poem by Phillis Wheatley." *New England Quarterly* 50 (1977): 517–20.

Lee, A. Robert. "Selves Subscribed: Early Afro-America and the Signifying of Phillis Wheatley, Jupiter Hammon, Olaudah Equiano and David Walker." *Making America/Making Amer-*

ican Literature. Eds. A. Robert Lee and W. M. Verhoeven. Amsterdam: Rodopi, 1996. 275–95.

Levernier, James A. "Phillis Wheatley (ca. 1753–1784)." *Legacy* 13.1 (1996): 64–75.

_____. "Phillis Wheatley and the New England Clergy." *Early American Literature* 26.1 (1991): 21–38.

_____. "Style as Protest in the Poetry of Phillis Wheatley." *Style* 27.2 (Summer 1993): 172–93.

_____. "Wheatley's 'On Being Brought from Africa to America.'" *Explicator* 40.1 (1981): 25–26.

Literature Criticism from 1400 to 1800: Critical Discussion of Fifteenth-, Sixteenth-, Seventeenth-, and Eighteenth-Century Novelists, Poets, Playwrights, Philosophers, and Other Creative Writers. 75 vols. Detroit: Gale Research Company, 1984.

Loggins, Vernon. *The Negro Author: His Development in America*. New York: Columbia University Press, 1931.

Long, Edward. *The History of Jamaica, or, General Survey of the Antient and Modern State of the*

Island: With Reflections on Its Situation Settlements, Inhabitants, Climate, Products, Commerce, Laws, and Government. London: T. Lowndes, 1774.

McKay, Michele, and William J. Scheick. "The Other Song in Phillis Wheatley's 'On Imagination.'" *Studies in the Literary Imagination* 27.1 (1994): 71–84.

Martin, Waldo. *The Mind of Frederick Douglass.* Chapel Hill: University of North Carolina Press, 1986.

Mason, Julian. "'Ocean': A New Poem by Phillis Wheatley." *Early American Literature* 34 (1999): 78–83.

Matson, R. Lynn. "Phillis Wheatley—Soul Sister?" *Phylon: The Atlanta University Review of Race and Culture* 33.3 (Fall 1972): 222–30.

Mphalele, Ezekiel. "From the Black American World: IV: Images of Africa in Afro-American Literature." *Okike, an African Journal of New Writing* 100 (1976): 98–99.

"The Nat Turner Insurrection." *The Anglo-African Magazine* 1.12 (1859): 225–38.

Newman, Richard, Patrick Rael, and Philip
    Lapsansky, eds. *Pamphlets of Protest: An An-
    thology of Early African American Protest Lit-
    erature, 1790–1860*. New York: Routledge,
    2001.

Nott, Walt. "From 'Uncultivated Barbarian' to
    'Poetical Genius': The Public Presence of
    Phillis Wheatley." *MELUS: The Journal of the
    Society for the Study of Multi-Ethnic Literature
    of the United States* 18 (1993): 21–32.

Odell, Margaretta Matilda. *Memoir and Poems of
    Phillis Wheatley*. Boston: Geo. W. Light, 1834.

Ogude, S. E. "Slavery and the African Imagina-
    tion: A Critical Perspective." *World Literature
    Today: A Literary Quarterly of the University of
    Oklahoma* 55.1 (1981): 21–25.

O'Neale, Sondra. "A Slave's Subtle War: Phillis
    Wheatley's Use of Biblical Myth and Sym-
    bol." *Early American Literature* 21.2 (1986):
    144–65.

_____. "Phillis Wheatley." *Dictionary of Literary
    Biography*. Ed. Emory Elliott. Vol. 31. De-
    troit: Gale Research Company, 1984. 360–67.

Oxley, Thomas. "Survey of Negro Literature." *Messenger: World's Greatest Negro Monthly* 60 (February 1927): 37–39.

Parks, Carole A. "Phillis Wheatley Comes Home." *Black World* 23.4 (1974): 92–97.

Peterson, Merrill D., ed. *The Portable Thomas Jefferson*. New York: Viking, 1975.

Porter, Dorothy Burnett, ed. *Early Negro Writing, 1760–1837*. Baltimore: Black Classic Press, 1997.

Prince, Dorothy Mains. "Phillis Wheatley: The Duplicity of Freedom." *Maryland Humanities* 78 (Summer 2001): 21–24.

Purvis, Robert. "*The National Anti-Slavery Standard*, Nov, 3, 1860." Sterling 265–66.

Quarles, Benjamin. "Antebellum Free Blacks and the 'Spirit of '76.'" *Journal of Negro History* 61.3 (1976): 229–42.

_____. *Black Mosaic: Essays in Afro-American History and Historiography*. Amherst: University of Massachusetts Press, 1988.

_____. "A Phillis Wheatley Letter." *Journal of Negro History* 34 (October 1949): 462–66.

Randall, Dudley. "Black Poetry." Gayle, *Black Expression* 109—114.

Redding, J. Saunders. "The Forerunners." Gayle, *Black Expression*: 63–65.

Reising, Russell. *Loose Ends: Closure and Crisis in the American Social Text*. Durham: Duke University Press, 1996.

Richards, Phillip M. "Phillis Wheatley, Americanization, the Sublime, and the Romance of America." *Style* 27.2 (Summer 1993): 194–221.

————. "Phillis Wheatley and Literary Americanization." *American Quarterly* 44.2 (1992): 163–91.

Richardson, William D. "Thomas Jefferson and Race: The Declaration of Independence and *Notes on the State of Virginia*." *Polity* XVI.3 (Spring 1984): 442–67.

Richmond, Merle A. *Bid the Vassal Soar: Interpretive Essays on the Life and Poetry of Phillis Wheatley (ca. 1753–1784) and George Moses Horton (ca. 1799–1883)*. Washington, D.C.: Howard University Press, 1974.

Rigsby, Gregory. "Form and Content in Phillis Wheatley's Elegies." *CLA Journal* 19 (December 1975): 248–57.

_____. "Phillis Wheatley's Craft as Reflected in Her Revised Elegies." *Journal of Negro Education* 47 (Fall 1978): 402–13.

Robinson, William H., ed. *Critical Essays on Phillis Wheatley*. Boston: G. K. Hall, 1982.

_____. *Phillis Wheatley: A Bio-Bibliography*. Boston: G. K. Hall, 1981.

_____. *Phillis Wheatley in the Black American Beginnings*. Detroit: Broadside Press, 1975.

_____. "Phillis Wheatley in London." *CLA Journal* 21 (December 1977): 187–201.

Rogal, Samuel J. "Phillis Wheatley's Methodist Connection." *Black American Literature Forum* 21.1–2 (1987): 85–95.

Scheick, William J. "Phillis Wheatley and Oliver Goldsmith: A Fugitive Satire." *Early American Literature* 19.1 (1984): 82–84.

_____. "Phillis Wheatley's Appropriation of Isaiah." *Early American Literature* 27.2 (1992): 135–40.

_____. "Subjection and Prophecy in Phillis Wheatley's Verse Paraphrases of Scripture." *College Literature* 22 (1995): 122–31.

Scruggs, Charles. "Phillis Wheatley and the Poetical Legacy of Eighteenth Century England." *Studies in Eighteenth-Century Culture* 10 (1981): 279–95.

Shields, David S. *Civil Tongues and Polite Letters in British America*. Chapel Hill: University of North Carolina Press, 1997.

Shields, John C. "Phillis Wheatley and Mather Byles: A Study in Literary Relationship." *CLA Journal* 23 (June 1980): 391–98.

_____. "Phillis Wheatley and the Sublime." Robinson, *Critical Essays* 189–205.

_____. "Phillis Wheatley's Subversion of Classical Stylistics." *Style* 27.2 (1993): 252–70.

_____. "Phillis Wheatley's Use of Classicism." *American Literature* 52 (March 1980): 97–111.

Shuffleton, Frank. "On Her Own Footing: Phillis Wheatley in Freedom." Carretta and Gould 175–89.

_____. "Phillis Wheatley, the Aesthetic, and the Form of Life." *Studies in Eighteenth-Century Culture* 26. Eds. Syndy M. Conger and Julie C. Hayes. Baltimore: Johns Hopkins University Press, 1998.

Silverman, Kenneth. *A Cultural History of the American Revolution: Painting, Music, Literature, and Theatre in the Colonies and the United States from the Treaty of Paris to the Inauguration of George Washington, 1763–1789.* New York: Columbia University Press, 1987.

_____. "Four New Letters by Phillis Wheatley." *Early American Literature* 8 (Winter 1974): 257–71.

Silvers, Anita. "Pure Historicism and the Heritage of Hero(in)es: Who Grows in Phillis Wheatley's Garden?" *Journal of Aesthetics and Art Criticism* 51.3 (1993): 475–82.

Sistrunk, Albertha. "The Influence of Alexander Pope on the Writing Style of Phillis Wheatley." Robinson, *Critical Essays* 175–88.

_____. "Phillis Wheatley: An Eighteenth-Century Black American Poet Revisited." *CLA Journal* 23 (June 1980): 391–8.

Smith, Cynthia J. "'To Maecenas': Phillis Wheatley's Invocation of an Idealized Reader." *Black American Literature Forum* 23.3 (Fall 1989): 579–91.

Smith, Eleanor. "Phillis Wheatley: A Black Perspective." *Journal of Negro Education* 43.3 (1974): 401–7.

Smith, James McCune. "On the Fourteenth Query of Thomas Jefferson's Notes on Virginia." *The Anglo-African Magazine* 1.8 (August 1859): 225–38.

_____. "Heads of the Colored People." *Frederick Douglass' Paper*. 25 March 1852: 1.

Stauffer, John. *The Black Hearts of Men: Radical Abolitionists and the Transformation of Race*. Cambridge: Harvard University Press, 2002.

Steele, Thomas J., S.J. "The Figure of Columbia: Phillis Wheatley Plus George Washington." *New England Quarterly* 54.2 (June 1981): 264–66.

Sterling, Dorothy, ed. *Speak Out in Thunder Tones: Letters and Other Writings by Black Northerners, 1787–1865*. New York: Da Capo Press, 1998.

Sterling, Eleonore Orland. "Thomas Jefferson and the Negro." *The Crisis* 59 (January 1952): 19–22.

Thatcher, B. B. *Memoir of Phillis Wheatley, A Native African and a Slave*. Boston: G. W. Light/New York: Moore and Payne, 1834.

Thurman, Wallace. "Negro Poets and Their Poetry." Gayle, *Black Expression*: 70–73.

Walker, Alice. "In Search of Our Mothers' Gardens: Honoring the Creativity of the Black Woman." *Jackson State Review* 6.1 (1974): 44–53.

Walker, Margaret, ed. Special Issue: The Phillis Wheatley Poetry Festival, November 4–7, 1974. *Jackson State Review* 6.1 (1974): 1–107.

Warren, Kenneth W. "Phillis Wheatley's Vision." *The New Yorker* 17–24 February 2003: 18.

Watson, Marsha. "A Classic Case: Phillis Wheatley and Her Poetry." *Early American Literature* 31.2 (1996): 103–32.

Whipper, William. "An Address Delivered in Wesley Church on the Evening of June 12, Before the Colored Reading Society of Philadelphia, For Mental Improvement" (Philadelphia: John Young, 1828). Porter 105–9.

Wilcox, Kirstin. "The Body into Print: Marketing Phillis Wheatley." *American Literature* 71.1 (March 1999): 1–29.

Willard, Carla. "Wheatley's Turns of Praise: Heroic Entrapment and the Paradox of Revolution." *American Literature* 67.2 (1995): 233–56.

Williams, Kenny J. "Phillis Wheatley." *Dictionary of Literary Biography*. Vol. 50. Eds. Trudier Harris and Thadious M. Davis. Detroit: Gale Research Company. 245–59.

Woodson, Carter G., ed. *The Mind of the Negro as Reflected in Letters Written During the Crisis: 1800–1860*. Washington, D.C.: The Association for the Study of Negro Life and History, Inc., 1926.

_____. "Thomas Jefferson's Thoughts on the Negro." *The Journal of Negro History* III.1 (January 1918): 55–89.

Wright, Richard. "Negro Literature in the United States." *White Man, Listen!* New York: Harper Perennial, 1995. 71–110.

Yarborough, Jean. "Race and the Moral Foundation of the American Republic: Another Look at the Declaration and the *Notes on Virginia*." *The Journal of Politics* 53.1 (February 1991): 90–105.

Yellin, Jean Fagan. *The Intricate Knot: Black Figures in American Literature, 1776–1863*. New York: New York University Press, 1972.

Index